D0931072

Books of Merit

WITH BORGES

WITH
BORGES

ALBERTO MANGUEL

Thomas Allen Publishers
Toronto

National Library of Canada Cataloguing in Publication

Manguel, Alberto, 1948–
    With Borges / Alberto Manguel.

ISBN 0-88762-146-5

1. Borges, Jorge Luis, 1899–   —Books and reading.
2. Borges, Jorge Luis, 1899–   —Friends and associates.
3. Manguel, Alberto, 1948–   —Friends and associates.
I. Title.

PS8576.A544Z478 2004   868'.6209   C004-900636-3

Editor: Jim Gifford
Jacket and text design: Gordon Robertson
Jacket images: Alamy Images
Photographs of Borges: Sara Facio

Published by Thomas Allen Publishers,
a division of Thomas Allen & Son Limited,
145 Front Street East, Suite 209,
Toronto, Ontario M5A 1E3 Canada

www.thomas-allen.com

  Canada Council
for the Arts

The publisher gratefully acknowledges the support of the
Ontario Arts Council for its publishing program.

We acknowledge the support of the Canada Council for the Arts,
which last year invested $20.3 million in writing and publishing
throughout Canada.

We acknowledge the Government of Ontario through the Ontario
Media Development Corporation's Ontario Book Initiative

We acknowledge the financial support of the Government of Canada
through the Book Publishing Industry Development Program (BPIDP)
for our publishing activities.

08 07 06 05 04   1 2 3 4 5

Printed and bound in Canada

For Héctor Bianciotti,
most generous of witnesses.

My memory carries me back to a certain
      evening . . .
in Buenos Aires. I see him; I see the gaslight;
      I could place
my hand on the shelves. I know exactly
      where to find
Burton's *Arabian Nights* and Prescott's
      Conquest of Peru,
though the library exists no longer.

— JORGE LUIS BORGES, *This Craft of Verse*

WITH BORGES

I shoulder my way through the crowds on Calle Florida, I enter the newly built Galería del Este, I come out on the other side and cross Calle Maipú and, leaning on the red marble façade of number 994, I press the button marked 6B. I enter the cool hall of the building and climb the six flights of stairs. I ring the bell and the maid opens, but almost before she can let me in, Borges appears from behind a heavy curtain, holding himself very straight, his grey suit buttoned up, his white collar and striped yellow tie slightly lopsided, shuffling a little as he comes towards me. Blind since his late fifties, he moves hesitantly even in a space he knows as well as this. His right hand reaches out and he welcomes me with a distracted boneless grip. There are no further formalities. He turns and leads the way into the living room and sits erect on the couch facing the entrance. I take a seat in the armchair to his right and he asks (but his questions are almost always rhetorical): "Well, shall we read Kipling tonight?"

For several years, from 1964 to 1968, I was fortunate enough to be among the many who read to Jorge Luis Borges. I worked after school in an Anglo-German bookstore in Buenos Aires, Pygmalion, where Borges was a frequent customer. Pygmalion was one of the meeting places for those interested in literature. The proprietor, Miss Lili Lebach, a German woman who had escaped the Nazi horrors, was keen on offering her clients the latest European and North American publications. She was an avid reader of literary supplements, not only of publishers' catalogues, and she had the gift of matching her finds with her customers' tastes. She taught me the need, for a bookseller, to know the wares he was selling, and she insisted that I read many of the new titles that came into the store. It did not take long to convince me.

Borges came to Pygmalion in the late afternoons, on his way back from his job as director of the National Library. One day, after picking up a couple of titles, he asked me, if I had nothing else to do, whether I would come and read to him in the evenings, since his mother, already in her nineties, became easily tired. Borges would ask almost anyone: students, journalists who came to interview him, other writers. There exists a vast group of those who once read out loud to Borges, minor Boswells whose identities are rarely known to one another but who collectively hold the memory of one of the world's great readers. I didn't know about them then.

I was sixteen years old. I accepted, and three or four times a week I would visit Borges in the small apartment he shared with his mother and with Fany, the maid.

In those days, I certainly was not aware of the privilege. My aunt, who admired him immensely, was slightly scandalized at my nonchalance and would urge me to take notes, to keep a journal of my encounters. But to me, those evenings with Borges were (in the arrogance of my adolescence) not really something extraordinary, something not alien to the world of books which I had always assumed was mine. If anything, it was most other conversations that seemed to me alien, uninteresting— conversations with my teachers about chemistry and the geography of the southern Atlantic, with my schoolmates about soccer, with my relatives about my exam results and my health, with neighbours about other neighbours. Instead, the conversations with Borges were what, in my

mind, conversations should always be: about books and about the clockwork of books, and about the discovery of writers I had not read before, and about ideas that had not occurred to me, or which I had glimpsed only in a hesitant, half-intuited way that, in Borges's voice, glittered and dazzled in all their rich and somehow obvious splendour. I didn't take notes because during those evenings I felt too contented.

From my very first visits, Borges's apartment seemed to me to exist outside time, or rather, in a time made up of Borges's literary experiences, a time composed of the cadenced eras of Victorian and Edwardian England, of the early Northern Middle Ages, of Buenos Aires of the twenties and thirties, of his beloved Geneva, of the age of German expressionism, of the loathed years of Perón, of the summers in Madrid and Majorca, of the months spent at the University of Austin, Texas, where he first received the generous admiration of the

United States. These were his points of reference, his history and his geography: the present seldom intruded. For a man who loved to travel but who could not see the places he visited (universities and foundations started inviting him regularly only after the mid-sixties), he was singularly uninterested in the physical world except as representations of his readings. The sand of the Sahara or the water of the Nile, the coast of Iceland, the ruins of Greece and Rome, all of which he touched with delight and awe, simply confirmed the memory of a page of the *Arabian Nights* or the Bible, of *Njals Saga* or of Homer and Virgil. All these "confirmations" he brought back to his apartment.

I remember the apartment as a muffled, warm, soft-scented place (due to the maid's insistence on keeping the heating up and of sprinkling *eau de cologne* on Borges's handkerchief before tucking it away, corners visible, into his jacket's breast pocket). It was fairly dark as well, and all these were features that seemed to suit the old man's blindness, creating a sense of happy isolation.

His was a particular kind of blindness, grown on him gradually since the age of thirty and settled in for good after his fifty-eighth birthday. It was a blindness expected since his birth, because he always knew that he had inherited feeble eyesight from his English great-grandfather and his grandmother, both of whom died blind. Also from his father, who had gone blind at about the same age as Borges, but who, unlike him, had recovered his sight after an operation, a few years before his death. Borges often talked about his own blindness, mainly with literary interest: famously, as a demonstration of the "irony of God" who had given him "books and the night"; historically, recalling celebrated blind poets such as Homer and Milton; superstitiously, since he was the third director of the National Library to be struck with blindness, after José Mármol and Paul Groussac; with almost scientific interest, lamenting not to be able to see any longer the colour black in the grey mist that surrounded him, and rejoicing in yellow, the only colour left to his eyes, the colour of his beloved tigers and of the roses he preferred, a fancy that caused friends to buy him loud yellow ties for every birthday and Borges to quote Oscar Wilde: "Only a deaf man could wear a tie like that"; in an elegiac mood, saying that blindness and old age were different ways of being alone. Blindness forced him into a solitary cell in which he composed his later work, building up lines in his head until they were ready to be dictated to whoever was at hand.

"Can you write this down?" He means the words he has just composed and which he has

learned by heart. He dictates them one by one, intoning the cadences he loves and speaking out the punctuation marks. He recites the new poem line by line, following not the sense on to the next verse, but breaking instead at the end of each line. Then he asks that it be read back to him, once, twice, five times. He apologizes for the request, but then asks again, listening to the words, turning them visibly in his mind. Then he adds another line, and another. The poem or the paragraph (because sometimes he takes the risk of writing prose again) takes shape on the paper as it has in his imagination. It is strange to think that the newborn composition appears for the first time in a handwriting that is not the author's. The poem is finished (a text in prose requires several days). Borges takes the piece of paper, folds it, places it in his wallet or inside a book. Curiously, he does the same with money. He takes a bill, folds it into a strip and places it inside one of the volumes of his library. Then, when he needs to pay for something, he pulls out a book and (sometimes, not always) finds the treasure.

In his apartment (as in the office he
occupied for many years at the National
Library), Borges sought the comfort of
routine, and nothing ever seemed to change
in the space he occupied. Every evening,
as I stepped behind the entrance curtain,
the layout of the apartment revealed itself
all at once. To the right, a dark table cov-
ered with a lace cloth and four straight-
backed chairs constituted the dining-room;
to the left, under a window, stood a well-
worn couch and two or three armchairs.
Borges would sit on the couch and I would
take one of the armchairs, facing him. His
blind eyes (they always had a melancholy
look, even when they wrinkled up in
laughter) would stare into a point in space
as he spoke, while my own eyes would
wander through the room, acquainting
myself once again with the familiar objects
of his daily life: a small table on which

he kept a silver mug and a *mate* that had belonged to his grandfather, a miniature writing desk dating from his mother's first communion, two white bookshelves set in the wall holding encyclopaedias, and two low bookcases of dark wood. On the wall hung a painting by his sister, Norah, depicting the Annuciation, and an engraving by Piranesi showing mysterious circular ruins. A short corridor to the far left led to the bedrooms: his mother's, full of old photographs, and his own, simple as a monk's cell. Sometimes, when we were about to leave for an evening walk or for dinner in the Hotel Dora across the road, the disembodied voice of Doña Leonor would reach us: "Georgie, don't forget your sweater, it might get cold!" Doña Leonor and Beppo, the big white cat, were two ghostly presences in that place.

I did not often see Doña Leonor. She was usually in her room when I arrived and only her voice would from time to time call out an instruction or a recommendation. Borges called her *madre* and she always used "Georgie," the English nickname that his Northumberland grandmother had given him.

Borges knew, from his earliest childhood, that he would be a writer, and his vocation was accepted as part of the family mythology. So much so that in 1909, Evaristo Carriego, a neighbourhood poet and friend of Borges's parents (and the subject of one Borges's first books), composed a few verses in honour of Doña Leonor's bookish ten-year old:

And that your son, the little child
Who makes you proud and now begins
To feel upon his head the mild
Longings for the laurel bough
Should, on the wing of reverie,
Carry on the harvesting
Of a second annunciation

Rendering the illustrious grapes
of the wine, the wine of Song.

Doña Leonor's relationship with her
famous son was predictably and fiercely
protective. Once, when she was being
interviewed on a French television documentary, she committed an unconscious
gaffe that would have delighted Dr Freud.
In answer to a question about acting as
Borges's secretary, she explained that she
had once assisted her blind husband and
that now she did the same for her blind
son. She meant to say *"J'ai été la main de
mon mari; maintenant, je suis la main de mon
fils"* ("I used to be my husband's hand,
now I'm the hand of my son") but, open-
ing the dyphtong in "main" as Spanish-
speaking people tend to do, she said instead:
*"J'ai été l'amant de mon mari; maintenant,
je suis l'amant de mon fils"* ("I used to be
my husband's lover, now I'm the lover of

my son"). Those who knew her posses-
siveness were not surprised.

His bedroom (sometimes he would ask
me to fetch a book there) was what mili-
tary historians call Spartan. An iron bed
with a white coverlet on which Beppo
would sometimes curl, a chair, a small desk
and two low bookcases were the only fur-
nishings. On the wall hung a wooden plate
with the coats of arms of the various can-
tons of Switzerland and Dürer's engraving
"Knight, Death and the Devil," which he
had celebrated in two rigorous sonnets.
According to his nephew, throughout his
life Borges repeated the same ritual before
falling sleep: he would wrestle into a long
white nightshirt and, closing his eyes, he
would recite out loud the Our Father in
English.

His world was wholly verbal: music,
colour and form rarely entered it. Borges
confessed many times that, as far as painting was concerned, he had always been

blind. He professed to like the work of his friend Xul Solar and of his sister, Norah Borges, and that of Dürer, Piranesi, Blake, Rembrandt, Turner, but these were literary, not iconographical loves. He criticized El Greco for peopling his heavens with dukes and archbishops ("A Paradise that resembles the Vatican: my idea of Hell . . .") and rarely commented on other painters. He also seemed deaf to music. He said he admired Brahms (one of his best stories is called "Deutsches Requiem") but he rarely listened to his music. From time to time, confronted with the music of Mozart, he would swear he was now converted, and that he could not understand how he had lived so long without Mozart; then he'd forget all about it, until his next epiphany. He would hum or sing tangos (the early ones) and *milongas*, but he detested Astor Piazzolla, who had so artfully renewed the music of Buenos Aires. The tango, according to Borges, had entered into decline

after 1910. In 1965, he wrote the words
to half a dozen *milongas*, but he said he
would never write the words to a tango.
"The tango comes late in the day, and to my
ears it is too sentimental, too close to French
tearjerkers like *Lorsque tout est fini* . . ." He
said he liked jazz. He remembered the
music that accompanied certain films, but
less for the music itself than for the way
in which it assisted the story, as in the case
of Bernard Hermann's score for *Psycho*, a
film he very much admired as "another
version of the doppelgänger, in which the
murderer becomes his mother, the person
he has murdered." He found this notion
mysteriously appealing.

He asks me if I will go with him to a film, a mu-
sical, West Side Story. *He has sat through it*
several times and never seems to tire of it. On the
way, he hums "Maria" and remarks on how true

*the fact that the name of the beloved changes
from a simple name to a divine utterance: Beat-
rice, Juliet, Lesbia, Laura. "Afterwards, everything is contaminated by that name," he says.
"Of course, perhaps it wouldn't have the same
effect if the name of the girl were Gumersinda,
eh? Or Bustefrieda. Or Bertha-aux-grands-
pieds, eh?" he chuckles. We sit in the cinema as
the lights go down. It is easier to sit with Borges
watching a film he has already seen, because
there is less to describe. From time to time, he
pretends he can see what is happening on the
screen, probably because someone has described it
to him on a previous sitting. He comments on
the epic quality of the rivalry between the gangs,
on the role of the women, on the use of the colour
red. Afterwards, as I walk him home, he talks of
cities who are themselves literary characters: Troy,
Carthage, London, Berlin. He could have added
Buenos Aires, to whom he has lent that kind of
bookish immortality. He loves walking down
the streets of Buenos Aires, at first, those of the
southern districts, later, through the crowded*

downtown where, like Kant in Königsberg, he became almost a feature of the landscape.

For a man who called the universe a library, and who confessed that he had imagined Paradise *"bajo la forma de una biblioteca,"* the size of his own library came as a disappointment perhaps because he knew, as he said in another poem, that language can only "imitate wisdom." Visitors expected a place overgrown with books, shelves bursting at the seams, piles of print blocking the doorways and protruding from every crevice, a jungle of ink and paper. Instead they would discover an apartment where books occupied a few unobtrusive corners. When the young Mario Vargas Llosa visited Borges sometime in the mid-fifties, he remarked on the quietly furnished surroundings and asked why the Master didn't live in a grander, more luxurious place.

Borges took great offence to this remark. "Maybe that's how they do things in Lima," he said to the indiscreet Peruvian, "but here in Buenos Aires we don't like to show off."

The few bookcases, however, contained the essence of Borges' reading, beginning with those that held the encyclopaedias and dictionaries, and were Borges' pride. "You know," he would say, "I like to pretend I'm not blind and I lust after books like a man who can see. I'm greedy for new encyclopaedias. I imagine I can follow the course of rivers on their maps and find wonderful things in the many entries." He liked to explain how, as a child, he would accompany his father to the National Library and, too timid to ask for a book, would simply take one of the volumes of the *Britannica* from the open shelves and read whatever article opened itself to his eyes. Sometimes he would be lucky, as when, he said, he chose volume *De–Dr* and learned about the Druids, the Druzes and

Dryden. He never abandoned this custom of trusting himself to the ordered chance of an encyclopaedia, and he spent many hours leafing through, and asking to be read from, the volumes of the *Bompiani*, the *Brockhaus,* the *Meyer, Chambers*, the *Britannica* (the eleventh edition, with essays by De Quincey and Macaulay, which he had bought with the money of a second-place Municipal Prize he received in 1928) or Montaner and Simón's *Diccionario Enciclopédico Hispanoamericano*. I would look up for him an article on Schopenhauer or Shintoism, Juana la Loca or the Scottish *fetch*. Then he would ask for a particularly appealing fact to be recorded, with the page number, at the back of the revelatory volume. Mysterious notations in a variety of hands sprinkled the end papers of his books.

The two low bookcases in the living-room held works by Stevenson, Chesterton, Henry James, Kipling. From here he took a small red, bound edition of *Stalky and Co.* with the head of the elephant god Ganesha and the Hindu swastika that Kipling had chosen as his emblem and which he removed during the War when the ancient symbol was co-opted by the Nazis; it was the copy Borges had bought in his adolescence in Geneva, the same copy he was to give me as a parting gift when I left Argentina in 1968. From here too he had me fetch the volumes of Chesterton's stories and Stevenson's essays, which we read over many nights and on which he commented with wonderful perspicacity and wit, not only sharing with me his passion for these great writers but also showing me how they worked by taking paragraphs apart with the amorous intensity of a clockmaker. Here too he kept J. W. Dunne's *An Experiment with Time*; several books by H. G. Wells; Wilkie Collins's *The Moonstone*; various novels by Eça de Queiroz in yellowing cardboard bindings; books by

Lugones, Güiraldes and Groussac; Joyce's
Ulysses and *Finnegans Wake*; *Vies Imaginaires*
by Marcel Schwob; detective novels by
John Dickson Carr, Milward Kennedy and
Richard Hull, Mark Twain's *Life on the
Mississippi*; Enoch Bennett's *Buried Alive*; a
small paperback edition of David Garnett's
Lady into Fox and *The Man in the Zoo*,
with delicate line illustrations; the more-
or-less *Complete Works* of Oscar Wilde
and the more-or-less *Complete Works* of
Lewis Carroll; Spengler's *Der Untergang
des Abend-landes*; the several volumes of
Gibbon's *Decline and Fall*; various books
on mathematics and philosophy, including
volumes by Swedenborg, Schopenhauer
and Borges's beloved *Wörterbuch der Philoso-
phie* by Fritz Mauthner. Several of these
books had accompanied Borges since his
adolescent days; others, the ones in English and German, carried the labels of the
Buenos Aires bookstores where they had

been bought, all now vanished: Mitchell's, Rodriguez, Pygmalion. He would tell visitors that Kipling's library (which he had visited) curiously held mainly non-fiction books, books on Asian history and travel, mainly on India. Borges concluded that Kipling had not wanted or needed the work of other poets or fiction writers, as if he had felt that his own creations sufficed for his own needs. Borges felt the contrary: he called himself above all a reader and it was the books of others that he wanted around him. He still had the large red, bound Garnier edition in which he had first read *Don Quixote* (a second copy, bought in his late twenties after the first one disappeared) but not the English translation of Grimm's *Fairy Tales*, the very first book he remembered reading.

The bookcases in his bedroom held volumes of poetry and one of the largest collections of Anglo-Saxon and Icelandic

literature in Latin America. Here Borges
kept the books he used to study what he
called

> the rough laborious words
> That with a mouth long turned to dust,
> I used in the day of Northumberland
>   and Mercia
> Before becoming Borges or Haslam.

A few I knew because I had sold them
to him at Pygmalion: Skeat's dictionary,
an annotated version of *The Battle of Mal-
don*, Richard Meyer's *Altgermanische Reli-
gions Geschichte*. The other bookcase held
the poems of Enrique Banchs, of Heine,
of San Juan de la Cruz, and many com-
mentaries on Dante: by Benedetto Croce,
Francesco Torraca, Luigi Pietrobono, Guido
Vitali.

Somewhere (perhaps in his mother's
bedroom) was the Argentine literature that

had accompanied the family on their voyage to Europe, shortly before World War I: Sarmiento's *Facundo*, *Siluetas militares* by Eduardo Gutiérrez, the two volumes of Argentine history by Vicente Fidel López, Mármol's *Amalia*, Eduardo Wilde's *Prometeo y Cía*, *Rosas y su tiempo* by Ramos Mejía, several volumes of poetry by Leopoldo Lugones. And the *Martín Fierro* by José Hernández, the Argentine national epic the adolescent Borges chose to take on board ship, a book Doña Leonor disapproved of because of its flashes of local colour and vulgar violence.

Absent from the apartment's bookshelves were his own books. He would proudly tell visitors who asked to see an early edition of one of his works that he didn't possess a single volume that carried his "eminently forgettable" name. Once, when I was visiting, the postman brought a large parcel containing a deluxe edition of his story "The Congress," published in

Italy by Franco Maria Ricci. It was a huge book, bound and cased in black silk with gold-leaf lettering and printed on hand-made blue Fabriano paper, each illustration (the story had been illustrated with Tantric paintings) hand-tipped and each copy numbered. Borges asked me to describe it. He listened carefully and then exclaimed: "But that's not a book, that's a box of chocolates!" and proceeded to make a gift of it to the embarrassed post-man.

Sometimes he himself chooses a book from the shelves. He knows, of course, where each volume is housed and he goes to it unerringly. But sometimes he finds himself in a place where the shelves are not familiar, in a foreign bookstore for instance, and here something uncanny happens. Borges will pass his hands over the spines of the books, as if feeling his way over the rugged sur-

face of a map in relief and, even if he does not know the territory, his skin seems to read the geography for him. Running his fingers over books he has never opened before, something like a craftsman's intuition will tell him what the book is that he is touching, and he is capable of deciphering titles and names which he certainly cannot read. (I once saw an old Basque priest work in this way among clouds of bees, able to tell them apart and assign them to different hives, and I also remember a park ranger in the Rockies who knew exactly in what part of the woods he found himself by reading the lichen on the tree trunks with his fingers.) I can vouch for the fact that there exists a relationship between this old librarian and his books which the laws of physiology would judge impossible.

For Borges, the core of reality lay in books: reading books, writing books, talking about books. In a visceral way, he was conscious of continuing a dialogue begun thousands of years ago and which he believed would never end. Books restored the past. "In time," he said to me, "every poem becomes an elegy." He had no patience with faddish literary theories and blamed French literature in particular for concentrating not on books but on schools and coteries. Adolfo Bioy Casares once told me that Borges was the only man he knew who, concerning literature, "never gave in to convention, custom or laziness." He was a haphazard reader who felt content, at times, with plot summaries and articles in encyclopaedias, and who confessed that, even though he had never finished *Finnegans Wake*, he happily lectured on Joyce's linguistic monument. He never felt obliged to read a book down to the last page. His library (which like that of every other reader was also his autobiography) reflected his belief in chance and the rules of anarchy. "I am a pleasure-seeking reader: I've never allowed my sense of duty to have a hand in such a personal matter as that of buying books."

This generous approach to literature (which he shared with Montaigne and Sir Thomas Browne and Lawrence Sterne) explains in turn his own appearance in so many different and scattered works now assembled under the common denominator of his presence: the first page of Michel Foucault's *Les mots et les choses*, which quotes a famous Chinese encyclopaedia (imagined by Borges) in which animals are divided into several incongruous categories, such as "those that belong to the Emperor" and "those that seen from afar resemble flies"; the character of the blind and criminal librarian who, under the name of Jorge de Burgos, haunts the monastic library in Umberto Eco's *The Name of the Rose*; the admiring and illuminating reference to Borges's 1932 text "The Translators of the Arabian Nights" in George Steiner's

seminal book on translation, *After Babel*;
the final lines of "A New Refutation of
Time," spoken by the dying machine in
Godard's *Alphaville*; Borges's features blend-
ing with those of Mick Jagger in the final
shot of Roeg and Cammell's failed 1968
film *Performance*; the encounter with the
Wise Old Man of Buenos Aires in Bruce
Chatwin's *In Patagonia* and in Nicholas
Rankin's *Dead Man's Chest*. During the last
few years of his life, he tried writing a story
called "Shakespeare's Memory" (which,
though he finally published, he never
judged to have achieved its purpose) about
a man who inherits the memory of the
author of Hamlet. From Foucault and
Steiner to Godard and Eco and the most
anonymous of readers, we have all inherited Borges's vast literary memory.

He remembered everything. He didn't
need copies of the books he had written:
though he pretended that they belonged

to the forgettable past, he could recite, correct and alter in his memory all of his own writings, usually to the stupefaction and delight of his listeners. Oblivion was a much-repeated wish (perhaps because he knew it was for him impossible) and forgetting, an affectation. He would tell a journalist that he no longer remembered his early work; the journalist, trying to flatter him, would quote a couple of ill-remembered lines from a poem, and Borges would quietly correct the misquotation and continue, by heart, the poem to the end. He had written a story, "Funes, el memorioso," which, he said, was "a long metaphor on insomnia." It was also a metaphor for his relentless memory. "My memory, sir," Funes tells the narrator, "is a rubbish heap." This "rubbish heap" allowed him to associate long-forgotten verses with other, better-known texts, and to enjoy certain writings because of a single word or because of the music of the language. Because of his colossal memory, all reading was, for him, rereading. His lips would move to the spoken words, mouthing the lines he had learned decades earlier. He remembered the lyrics of old tangos; atrocious verses by long-dead poets; snatches of dialogues and descriptions from all kinds of novels and stories, riddles and one-liners; long poems in English, German, Spanish, and also in Portuguese and Italian; quips and puns and limericks; lines from the Northern sagas; injurious anecdotes about people he knew; passages from Virgil. He said he admired inventive memories, like that of De Quincey, which could transform a German translation of a few lines of Russian verse on the Tartars of Siberia into seventy splendidly "remembered" pages, or that of Andrew Lane who, when retelling the Aladdin story from the *Arabian Nights*, "recalled" Aladdin's evil uncle putting his ear to the ground and hearing the footsteps of his enemy on the other side of the earth—an episode the *Arabian Nights'* author never imagined.

Sometimes, a memory comes to him, and more for his own amusement than for mine, he begins to tell a story and ends with a confession. Discussing the "cult of courage," as he calls the code of the street toughs of Buenos Aires at the turn of the century, Borges remembers that a certain Soto, a professional bruiser, is told by the tavern keeper that there is another man in town, carrying his same name. The other happens to be a lion tamer, a member of an itinerant circus which had come to the neighbourhood to give a performance. Soto enters the tavern where the lion tamer is having a drink and asks the man his name. "Soto," the lion tamer answers. "The only Soto around here is me," says the bruiser, "so grab a knife and step outside." The terrified lion tamer is forced to comply and is killed

*because of a code he knows nothing about.
"That episode," Borges tells me, I stole for the
ending of my story "The South."*

If he had a favourite literary genre (he dis-
believed in literary genres) it was the epic.
In the Anglo-Saxon sagas, in Homer, in
the gangster films and westerns of Holly-
wood, in Melville and in the mythology of
the Buenos Aires underworld, he recognized the same themes of courage and
battle. For Borges, the epic theme is
an essential hunger, like that for love or
happiness, or misfortune. "All literatures
begin by the epic," he would say in its
defence, "not by any intimate or sentimental poetry." And he would quote the
Odyssey to explain this: "The gods weave
adversities for men so that future generations will have something to sing about."
Epic poetry brought tears to his eyes.

He loved the German language. He had taught it to himself at the age of seventeen in Switzerland, during the long nights of curfew imposed by the war, reading his way through the poems of Heine. "Once you know the meaning of *Nachtigall, Liebe, Herz,* you can read Heine without the help of a dictionary," he said. And he enjoyed the possibilities German allowed of making up words, as Goethe's *Nebelglanz,* "the glimmer of the fog." He would let the words resound in the room: *"Füllest wieder Busch und Thal still mit Nebelglanz . . ."* He praised the transparency of the language, and he reproached Heidegger for having invented what he called "an incomprehensible dialect of German."

He loved detective novels. He found in their formulae the ideal narrative structures which allow the fiction writer to set up his own borders and to concentrate on the efficiency of words and images made of words. He enjoyed significant details. He once observed, as we were reading the Sherlock Holmes story "The Red-Headed League," that detective fiction was closer to the Aristotelian notion of a literary work than any other genre. According to Borges, Aristotle had stated that a poem about the labours of Hercules would not have the unity of the *Illiad* or the *Odyssey*, since the only uniting factor would be the single same hero undertaking the various labours, and that in the detective story the unity is given by the mystery itself.

He was not above melodrama. He would cry at westerns and gangster films. He sobbed at the ending of *Angels with Dirty Faces* when James Cagney behaves as a coward when they take him to the electric chair so the boys who idolize him will not look up to him any longer. Standing on the edge of the pampas, the sight of which he said affected Argentines as the sight of the sea affected the English, a tear would roll down his cheek and he would mutter: *"Carajo, la patria!"* ("By God, my homeland!"). His breath would stop when he would come to the line the Norwegian sailor says to his king as the mast of the royal ship cracks: "That was Norway breaking/ from thy hand, O king!" (in a poem by Longfellow, a line—Borges pointed out— then used by Kipling in "The Most Beautiful Story in the World"). He once recited the Our Father in Old English, in a crumbling Saxon chapel near Dr Johnson's Lichfield, "to give God a little surprise." He wept at a certain paragraph by the forgotten Argentinian writer Manuel Peyrou because it mentioned Calle Nicaragua, a street close to where Borges was born. He enjoyed reciting four verses by Rubén Darío, *"Boga y boga en el lago sonoro/ que en el sueño a los tristes espera/ donde aguarda una góndola de oro/ a la novia de Luis de Baviera,"*

because in spite of the long vanished gon-
dolas and royal brides, the rhythm brought
tears to his eyes. He confessed many times
that he was unabashedly sentimental.

But he could also be pointedly cruel.
Once, as we were sitting in the living
room, a writer whose name I don't want
to remember came to read to Borges a
story he had written in his honour.
Because it dealt with knifers and hoodlums, he thought Borges would enjoy it.
Borges prepared himself to listen; the hands
on the cane, the slightly parted lips, the
eyes staring upwards suggested, to someone who did not know him, a sort of
polite meekness. The story was set in a
tavern filled with low-life characters. The
neighbourhood police inspector, known
for his bravery, comes in unarmed and
merely through the authority of his voice
forces the men to give up their weapons.
Then the writer, with enthusiasm, began
listing them: "A dagger, two revolvers,

one leather cosh . . ." Borges picked up
in his deadly monotone voice: ". . . three
rifles, one bazooka, a small Russian can-
non, five scimitars, two machetes, a mean
pop-gun . . ." The writer managed a small
laugh. But Borges continued relentlessly:
"three sling shots, one brickbat, an arbal-
est, five poleaxes, one battering ram . . ."
The writer stood up and wished us good-
night. We never saw him again.

*On occasion he tires of being read to, he becomes
weary of books, of literary conversations that he
repeats with slight variations with every occa-
sional visitor. He then likes to imagine a universe in which magazines and books are not
necessary because every man is capable of every
magazine and book, of every story and every
line of verse. In this universe (he will describe
it eventually under the title "Utopia of a Tired
Man"), every man is an artist and therefore art is*

*no longer necessary: gone are galleries, libraries,
museums; vanished the names of individuals
and countries; everything wonderfully anonymous, no book a failure or a success. He agrees
with Cioran who, in an article on Borges, lamented
that fame had finally unearthed the secret writer
he once was.*

We studied him in school. By the sixties he
had not acquired the universal fame of his
later years, but he was considered among
the "classic" Argentine writers, and teachers dutifully led their classes through the
labyrinths of his fictions and the precise-
ness of his poems. Studying Borges's writing in grammatical detail (we were set
paragraphs from his stories to analyze syn-
tactically) was a mysteriously fascinating
exercise, the closest I ever came to under-
standing something of how his verbal imagination worked. Unravelling a sentence

showed us how simple, how clean his work-
ings were, how efficiently verbs accorded
with nouns and clauses fit into clauses. His
use of adjectives and adverbs, a use which
grew increasingly sparse as he grew older,
created new senses out of commonplace
words, less astonishing in their novelty
than in their justness. A long line such as
the one beginning "The Circular Ruins"
(a story the poet Alejandra Pizarnik could
recite from beginning to end, by heart,
like a poem) creates a setting, a mood, a
dreamlike reality through the repetition of
a noun and the punctuation of a few surprising epithets: *"Nadie lo vio desembarcar en
la unánime noche, nadie vio la canoa de bambú
sumiéndose en el fango sagrado, pero a los pocos
días nadie ignoraba que el hombre taciturno
venía del Sur y que su patria era una de las in-
finitas aldeas que están aguas arriba, en el flanco
violento de la montaña, donde el idioma zend
no está contaminado de griego y donde es infre-
cuente la lepra."* The geographical space

is inhabited by that witnessing Nobody; "unanimous" joined to "night" and "sacred" to "mud" produce an overwhelming darkness and a sense of holy terror; the South defined through the word "violent" (as in "rough") applied to the mountainside and through two further absences: that of the contaminating Greek tongue and of the archetypal dreaded sickness. Little wonder that, in my book-haunted adolescence, lines like this one would come back to me just before falling asleep, like an incantation.

The truth was that Borges renewed the Spanish language. Partly, his generous reading methods allowed him to bring into Spanish felicities from other tongues: English turns of phrase or the German ability to hold until the end of a sentence its subject. Either writing or translating, he used the freedom of his common sense to alter or prune a text. For instance, attempting to produce a never-to-be-completed Spanish version of *Macbeth* with Bioy Casares, he suggested transforming the famous summons of the witches ("When shall we three meet again/ In thunder, lightning, or in rain?") into *"Cuando el fulgor del trueno otra vez/ seremos una sola cosa las tres"* ("When the thunder shines/ Again we three shall become one"). "If you are going to translate Shakespeare," he said, "you must do it as freely as Shakespeare wrote. We invented therefore a sort of diabolical Trinity for his three witches."

Since the seventeenth century, Spanish writers had hesitated between the linguistic poles of Góngora's baroque and Quevedo's severity; Borges developed for himself both a rich, multi-layered vocabulary of new poetic meanings and a deceptively simple, bare-boned style which (he said late in his career) attempted to mirror that of the young Kipling of *Plain Tales from the Hills*. Almost every major writer in Spanish, this century, has acknowledged a debt to Borges, from Gabriel García

Márquez to Julio Cortázar, from Carlos Fuentes to Severo Sarduy, and his literary voice echoed so strongly in the writings of the younger generations that the Argentinian novelist Manuel Mujica Láinez was moved to write the following quatrain:

A un joven escritor

Inútil es que te forjes
Idea de progresar
Porque aunque escribas la mar
Antes lo habrá escrito Borges.

By the age of thirty he had discovered everything, even the Anglo-Saxon sagas which would occupy so much of his studies in later years: already in 1932 he had explored these distant literatures in "The Kennigar," a meditation on the artificiality and effect of metaphors. He remained faithful to the subjects of his youth: he returned to them over and over again, through

decades of distillation, interpretation, re-interpretation.

His language (and the style in which he wrote that language) came largely from reading, and from translating into Spanish authors such as Chesterton and Schwob. Partly it came from everyday conversation, from the civilized habit of sitting at a café table or over dinner with friends and discussing the great eternal questions with humour and ingenuity. He had a gift for the paradox, the quiet and illuminating turn of phrase, the elegant nonsense such as his admonition to his nephew, aged five or six: "If you behave, I'll give you permission to think of a bear."

He had no patience with stupidity and he once said, after meeting a particularly dull-headed university professor: "I'd prefer to converse with an intelligent scoundrel." There has always been, in Argentina, a national inclination to converse, to put life into words. In other societies the

discussion of metaphysics over a cup of
coffee may seem pretentious or absurd;
not so in Argentina. Borges loved conversation and at meals would select what he
called "unobtrusive fare," white rice or
pasta, so that the experience of eating
would not distract him from the talk. He
believed that what any man has experi-
enced every man can experience, and as a
young man, he was not surprised to find,
among his father's friends, a writer who, all
on his own, had rediscovered the ideas of
Plato and other philosophers. Macedonio
Fernández wrote little, read little, but
thought much and conversed brilliantly.
He became, for Borges, the incarnation of
pure thought: a man who, throughout long
conversations in a café, would ask and attempt to solve the old metaphysical questions about time and existence, dreams and
reality, which Borges was later to make
his in book after book. With the politeness
of Socrates, he would offer his listeners

the paternity of his own ideas. He would
say: "You will have noticed, Borges . . . ,"
or "You will have realized, So-and-So . . . ,"
and then he would attribute to So-and-So
or to Borges a discovery he had just made.
Macedonio had a fine sense of the absurd
and a cutting humour. Once, to dismiss an
enthusiast of Victor Hugo, whom Macedonio found long-winded, he exclaimed:
"Victor Hugo, come on, that unbearable
dago! The reader's gone away and he keeps
on talking." Another time, when asked
if there had been a large attendance to a
certain forgettable cultural event, Macedonio answered: "So many were absent that
if one more hadn't come he wouldn't have
been able to get in." (Alas, the authorship
of this celebrated *bon mot* is in dispute . . .
According to Borges, it was coined by
a cousin of his, Guillermo Juan Borges,
"inspired" by Macedonio.) Borges always
remembered Macedonio as the archetypal
inhabitant of Buenos Aires.

From the baroque richness of one of his first books, *Evaristo Carriego*, to the laconic tones of stories such as "Death and the Compass" (set in a pseudonymous city) and "The Dead Man," and the later long fable "The Congress," Borges constructed for Buenos Aires a cadence and a mythology with which the city is now identified. When Borges began writing, Buenos Aires (so far from Europe, the perceived centre of culture) felt vague and indistinct, and seemed to require a literary imagination to impose it upon reality. Borges recalled that when the now forgotten French writer Anatole France visited Argentina in the 1920s, Buenos Aires felt "a little more real" because Anatole France knew that it existed. Now Buenos Aires feels more real because it exists in Borges's pages. The Buenos Aires Borges proposed to his readers is rooted in the neighbourhood of Palermo, where stood the family house; beyond the garden railings, Borges set his stories and poems of *compadritos*, local hoodlums whom he saw as low-life warriors and poets, and in whose violent lives he heard modest echoes of the *Iliad* and the ancient Viking sagas. The Buenos Aires of Borges is also the metaphysical centre of the world: on the nineteenth step leading to the cellar of Beatriz Viterbo's house the Aleph can be seen, the point in which the entire universe is concentrated; the old National Library on Calle Mexico is the Library of Babel; the polished furniture and dark mirrors of the ancient mansions of Borges's Palermo threaten the reader who stares into them with the horror that one day they will reflect a face that will not be his; the tiger at the Buenos Aires zoo stands as a burning symbol of the perfection the writer must always be denied, even in dreams.

Tigers were his emblematic beast, from his early childhood. "What a pity not to have been born a tiger," he once said as we were reading a story by Kipling which featured the ghost of the beast. His mother remembered dragging him away screaming, at the age of three or four, from the tiger's cage, when it was time to go home, and one of his first scribbles that she kept was of a striped tiger, drawn in coloured crayons over a double page of a scrapbook. Later on, the spots of a jaguar seen in the Buenos Aires zoo caused him to imagine a system of writing printed onto the jaguar's coat: the result was the splendid story "The Writing of the God." A mention of tigers would lead him to quote an observation made by his sister Norah when they were children: "Tigers seem to have been created for love." A few months before he died, a rich Argentine landowner invited Borges to his *estancia* and promised "a surprise." He sat the old man on a bench in the garden, left him there and suddenly Borges felt a large warm body next to him, and large paws resting on his shoulders.

The *estanciero*'s pet tiger had paid homage
to his dreamer. Borges was unafraid. Only
the hot breath that stank of raw meat
bothered him. "I had forgotten that tigers
are carniverous."

We take a taxi to Bioy and Silvina's place, a
vast apartment overlooking a park. For decades
now, Borges has spent several evenings every
week at their apartment. The food is terrible—
boiled vegetables and a spoonful of dulce de leche
(milk jam) for dessert, but Borges never notices.
Tonight, each in turn, Bioy Casares, Silvina
Ocampo and Borges recall their dreams for one
another. Silvina, in a deep and quaky voice,
mentions that she had dreamt that she was
drowning, but that the dream was not a night-
mare: she wasn't in pain, she wasn't afraid, she
merely felt that she was dissolving, turning into
water. Bioy then mentions that he dreamt that
he found himself in front of a set of double doors.

He knew, with the certainty one sometimes feels in dreams, that the door to the right would lead him to a nightmare; he stepped through the door to his left and had an uneventful dream. Borges observes that both dreams, Silvina and Bioy's, are in some sense identical, since both dreamers succeeded in avoiding the nightmare, one by giving in to it, the other by refusing to enter it. He then recalls a dream described by Boetius. In the dream, Boetius is watching a horse race: he sees the horses, the start of the race, the different and successive moments until one of the horses reaches the finish line. But then Boetius sees another dreamer: one who sees him, the horses, the race, all at once, in a single instant. For that dreamer, who is God, the outcome of the race is up to the riders, but that outcome has already been known by God the Dreamer. For God, Borges says, Silvina's dream would be both pleasant and a nightmare, Bioy's dream would entail walking through both doors at the same time. "For that colossal dreamer, each dream is equivalent to eternity, which contains every dream and every dreamer."

Borges met Bioy in 1930, when Victoria Ocampo, the formidable *dame des lettres*, introduced the shy thirty-one-year-old Borges to the brilliant seventeen-year-old. Their friendship, Borges was to say, became the most important relationship in Borges's life, providing him not only with an intellectual partner but with someone who would temper Borges's delight in hard-edged imagination with a keener interest in the psychology and social circumstances of his literature. Borges played with irony and understatement; Bioy with a deceptive naïveté that leads the reader to believe that the intentions of a certain character reflect the truth of a situation when in fact they betray or ignore it. Borges summed up his friend's method at the beginning of "Tlön Uqbar, Orbis Tertius" (a story in which Bioy appears as a character): "Bioy Casares had dined with me that night and we were delayed by a long discussion concerning the writing of a novel in the first person, whose narrator would omit or alter the facts and incur in various contradictions that would allow a few readers—very few readers—to guess the existence of a terrible or trivial reality." "I would like," Borges said, "to write a story that had the quality of a dream. I've tried. I don't think I've ever succeeded."

Borges was a keen dreamer, and enjoyed telling his dreams. Here, in "that all-possible realm," he felt that he could release the hold on his thoughts and fears, and that they could, in all freedom, act out their own stories. He enjoyed particularly the minutes which preceded sleep, that time between sleep and wakefulness in which,

he said, he was "conscious of losing consciousness." "I say meaningless words to myself, I see unknown places, I let myself slide down *the slope of dreams*." Sometimes a dream would give him a clue or a starting point for a story: "The Memory of Shakespeare," for instance, began with a line he heard in dream: "I will sell you the memory of Shakespeare." "The Circular Ruins" (the story of a man who dreams another, only to discover that he himself is a dream) began in yet another dream and led to a week of complete rapture—the only time, he said, he had felt truly "inspired" and not in conscious control of his creation. (I also believe that the story, and perhaps the dream, was inspired by a memory of the *Aeneid*, since Aeneas's landing in the dream-world of the dead "amidst wan reeds on a dreary mud flat" is surely the same as that of the dreamer on the island of Circular Ruins.)

Two nightmares haunted Borges throughout his life: of mirrors and the labyrinth. The labyrinth, first discovered as a child in a copperplate engraving of the Seven Marvels of the World, made him fear "a house with no doors" at the centre of which a monster awaited him; mirrors terrified him with the suspicion that one day they would reflect back a face that was not his, or worse, no face at all. Hector Bianciotti recalls that, as Borges lay sick in Geneva shortly before his death, he asked Marguerite Yourcenar, who had gone to visit him, to find the apartment his family had occupied during their stay in Switzerland, and come back and describe it to him as it now stood. She complied, but she left out of her description one detail: now, when someone entered the apartment, a gigantic mirror in a golden frame reflected the surprised visitor from head to foot. Yourcenar spared Borges that nightmarish intrusion.

Bioy was certainly one of those numerous men that Borges knew he would never be: the old man's intellectual partner but also handsome, rich and an accomplished sportsman. When Borges wrote, "I, who have been so many men, have never been the one in whose arms Mathilde Urbach swooned," he might have been thinking of Bioy, the ladykiller. Bioy never disguised the fact that women were his passion, together with books (if his posthumous diaries are anything to go by, more than books). For Borges, knowledge of love was to be found in literature, in the words of Shakespeare's Anthony, and of Kipling's soldier in "Without Benefit of Clergy," in the poems of Swinburne and Enrique Banchs. For Bioy, it was a daily exercise to which he dedicated himself with the devotion of a lepidopterist. He would quote Victor Hugo, *"aimer c'est agir,"* but he added that this was a truth to be hidden from women. He loved France and French

literature as much as Borges loved England
and the literature of the Anglo-Saxons.
This was not a parting issue but the beginning of many conversations. In fact, everything between these two men seemed to
lead to an exchange of words. Working
together in one of the back rooms of Bioy's
apartment, they reminded me of alchemists
putting together a homunculus, creating
something that was a combination of features of both and yet was unlike either of
them. In that new voice which was neither
as satirical as that of Bioy nor as cerebral as
that of Borges, they composed the stories
and mock essays of H. Bustos Domecq,
an Argentine gentleman of letters who
looked with a seemingly innocent eye at
the absurdities of Argentine society. Bustos
Domecq particularly delighted in the quirks
and hideous turns of the Argentine language; one of his stories carries as an epi-
graph merely the quotation's source: Isaiah,
VI, 5. The curious (or knowledgeable) reader

will discover that the quotation itself reads: "Then said I, Woe is me! for I am undone; because I am a man of unclean lips, and I dwell in the midst of a people of unclean lips . . ." Bioy would share with Borges the things he heard among the "people of unclean lips" and they would burst out laughing.

The relationship with Silvina was different. Over dinner, Borges and Bioy would recall, embroider and invent a vast array of literary anecdotes, recite passages from the best and the worst of literature and essentially have a great time, laughing uproariously. Silvina would contribute only occasionally to the dialogue. Though she had compiled, together with Bioy and with Borges, an essential anthology of fantastic literature in Spanish translation, and had written a detective novel with Bioy, *Those Who Love, Hate*, her literary sensibilities were clearly different from theirs, closer to the black humour of the surrealists for whom Borges had little sympathy. Borges, oddly enough for someone who admired gangsters and hoodlums, found her stories too cruel. Silvina was a poet, a playwright and a painter, but no doubt she will be remembered for her sardonic and deceivingly simple short stories, most of which belong to the realm of fantastic literature but which she constructed with the minute attention of a chronicler of ordinary life. Italo Calvino, who wrote the introduction for the Italian edition of her work, confessed that he didn't know of another writer "who better captures the magic of everyday rituals, the forbidden face that our mirrors don't show us."

One evening, while Bioy and Borges were working away in one of the back rooms from which, every so often, shouts of shared laughter would erupt, Silvina pulled down a copy of the *Alice* books and read a few favourite sections in her cadenced, lugubrious voice. In the middle of "The Walrus and the Carpenter," she suddenly suggested that she and I collaborate on a fantastic thriller for which she had found the perfect title, taken from the oysters' plea: *A Dismal Thing to Do*. The project never proceeded beyond the planning of a gruesome murder, but led to long discussion about the humour of Emily Dickinson; the influence of detective fiction on the work of Franz Kafka; whether literature can be modernized through translation; the fact that Andrew Marvel had only written one good poem; the advice Giorgio De Chirico had given her when he had taught her to paint, that a painter must never show the brushstrokes; the curiously awful love song by Pablo Neruda that begins, "*Eras la boina gris*"—"You were the grey beret and the heart at peace" (Silvina kept repeating "*boina, boina* " and asking, in her deep and fluttery voice: "Do you *like* that word?"). During the conversation, in which she did most of the talking in a sort of incantatory rhythm that haunted one for many hours afterwards, she would keep her face in the shade and her eyes behind thick dark glasses because she felt that she had ugly features, and would try to draw one's attention to her beautiful legs which she crossed and uncrossed incessantly.

Borges never thought of Silvina as his intellectual equal: her interests and her writings were too far removed from his. Her poems have something of Emily Dickinson and something of Ronsard; her themes, however, were uniquely her own: the unwieldy country she loved, and the gardens of the city, and also the small moments of happiness, bewilderment, revenge. Her paintings—mainly portraits—have the flat surfaces and colours of de Chirico, but she did strange things to the sitters' eyes so that they seem to reveal something dark and forbidden. Her stories describe an everyday supernatural: a dying woman is suddenly confronted with all the objects she has possessed in the past and made to realize that they constitute her private hell; a boy invites to his birthday party the seven deadly sins in the guise of seven little girls; a child is abandoned in a lovers' motel and becomes the unwitting instrument of a woman's revenge; two schoolboys exchange their destinies and nevertheless can't escape them. In most of her fiction, her heroes are children and animals, in both of whom she recognized an intelligence beyond reason. She loved dogs. When her favourite dog died, Borges found her in tears and tried to console her by telling her that there was a Platonic dog beyond all dogs, and that every dog was The Dog. Silvina was furious and in no uncertain terms told him to go stuff it.

In the last years of her life (she died in 1993, aged eighty-eight) she suffered from Alzheimer's and wandered through her large apartment unable to remember where or who she was. One day, a friend found her reading a book of stories. Full of enthusiasm, she told the friend (whom, of course she didn't recognize, but by then she had grown accustomed to the presence of strangers) that she would read him something wonderful which she had just discovered. It was a story from one of her first and most famous books, *Autobiography of Irene*. The friend listened and told her she was right. It was a masterpiece.

Borges speaks not so much of being friends with the writers he knows but as being their reader, as if they belonged not to the everyday world but to the world of the library. Even in the realm of friendship, the role of the reader predominates. The reader, not the writer. He believes that the reader takes over the writer's task. "You can't know if a poet is good or bad without having some idea of what he proposed

to do," he tells me, as we walk down Calle
Florida, stopping wherever the quotation requires
it, as the hurried crowds walk past us, many rec-
ognizing the old blind man of Buenos Aires.
"And if I can't understand a poem, I can't know
what the intention was." He then quotes a line
from Corneille, a writer he does not admire, and
praises the fine oxymoron: "Cette obscure
clarté qui tombe des étoiles." *"Good," he*
says. "Now we're a bit Corneille." And he
laughs and starts walking again. Corneille or
Shakespeare, Homer or the soldiers of Hastings:
reading is, for Borges, a way to be all those men
he knew he'll never be: men of action, great
lovers, great warriors. For him, reading is a
form of pantheism, that ancient philosophical
school that had interested Spinoza. I mention
his story "The Immortal," in which Homer
lives throughout the centuries, unable to die and
under various names. Borges stops walking
again and says: "The pantheists imagined the
world as inhabited by only one person, God,
and God is dreaming all the world's creatures,

*including us. In this philosophy, we are the
dreams of God, and we don't know it." And
then: "But does God know little bits of Him are
now walking among crowds down this Calle
Florida?" And stopping once more: "But maybe
that is no concern of ours."*

His concern was literature, and no writer,
in this vociferous century, was as important in changing our relationship to literature as he was. Perhaps other writers were
more adventurous, keener in their travel-
ling through our secret geographies. No
doubt there were those who documented
more powerfully than he ever did our social
miseries and rituals, as there were those
who ventured more successfully into the
Amazonian regions of our psyche. Borges
attempted little or nothing of all this. Instead, throughout his long life, he drew maps
for us to read those other explorations—

especially in the realm of his favourite literary genre, the fantastic, which in his books included religion, philosophy and higher mathematics. He read theology with keen enjoyment. "I'm the contrary of the Argentine Catholic," he told me. "They believe but are not interested; I'm interested, but I don't believe." He admired Saint Augustine's metaphoric use of Christian symbols. "The cross of Christ has saved us from the circular labyrinth of the stoics," he would quote Augustine with delectation. And then add: "But I still prefer that circular labyrinth."

Even reading books on religion or philosophy, what interested him was the literary voice which, for Borges, had always to be individual, never national, never of a group or a school of thought. He would recall Valéry, who longed for a literature with no dates, no names, no nationalities, in which all writings would be seen as creations of the same spirit, the Holy

Ghost. "At the university, we don't study literature," he would complain. "We study the history of literature."

In spite of himself, Borges changed forever the notion of literature and consequently that of the history of literature. In a famous text whose first version was published in 1952, he wrote: "Every writer creates his own precursors." With this statement, Borges adopted a long lineage of writers who now appear Borgesian *avant la lettre*: Plato, Novalis, Kafka, Schopenhauer, Rémy de Gourmont, Chesterton . . . Even writers who seem beyond all individual claim, classics among classics, now belong to Borges's reading, like Cervantes after Pierre Menard. To a reader of Borges, even Shakespeare and Dante ring at times with a distinct Borgesian echo: the Provost's line in *Measure for Measure* about being "insensible of mortality, and desperately mortal," and that verse in the fifth canto of *Purgatorio* that describes Buonconte *"fugendo a pede e sanguinando il piano"* are most certainly in Borges's hand.

In "Pierre Menard, author of *Don Quixote*" he argued that a book changes according to the reader's attributions. When the text first appeared in *Sur* in May 1939, several readers assumed that Pierre Menard was real; one such reader even went as far as telling Borges that there was nothing new in what he had outlined, that it had all been noted by previous writers. Pierre Menard is, of course, an invention, a superb and hilarious imagination, but the notion of a text that changes according to the reader's assumptions is old. From fakes such as Macpherson's Ossian, over whose verses Werther wept as if they belonged to an ancient Celtic bard, to the "real life" adventures of Robinson Crusoe and Sir John Mandeville, which led enthusiasts of archeological truth to explore the Island of Juan Fernández and to unearth the ruins of what might have been Cathay; from the

"Song of Songs" studied as a sacred text to *Gulliver's Travels* catalogued dismissively as a children's book, readers have always read according to their own beliefs and desires. In "Pierre Menard" Borges merely extends this idea to its ultimate conclusion, and fixes the fluid concept of authorship firmly in the realm of he who rescues the words from the page. After Borges, after the revelation that it is the reader who in fact gives life and title to literary works, the notion of literature as merely the author's creation became impossible. For Borges, this "death of the author" was not a tragic event. He amused himself with such subversions. "Imagine," he would say, "reading Don Quixote as if it were a detective novel. *En un lugar de la Mancha, de cuyo nombre no quiero acordarme* . . . The author tells us he doesn't want to remember the name of the village. Why? What clue is he concealing? As readers of a detective novel

we are meant to suspect something, no?"
And he would laugh.

Another of Borges's subversions is the
notion that every book, any book, holds
the promise of all others, both mechani-
cally and intellectually. Borges believed
this to be true, provided that the idea could
be taken to its uttermost limits. Every text
is a combination of the twenty-four letters
of the alphabet (more or less, according to
each language). For that reason, an infinite
combination of these letters would give
us a complete library of every conceivable
book past, present and future: "the metic-
ulous history of the future, the auto-
biographies of the archangels, the faithful
catalogue of the library, thousands and
thousands of false catalogues, the demonstration that such catalogues are false, the
demonstration that the real catalogue is
in fact false, the gnostic gospel of Basil-
ides, the commentary on that gospel, the

commentary on the commentary, the true account of your death, the translation of every book into every language, the interpolation of every book into every other book, the treatise the Venerable Bede was unable to write (and indeed did not write) on the mythology of the Saxons, the lost books of Tacitus." This, in "The Library of Babel," of which he wrote a first version in 1939.

The reverse is also true. The infinite library can be considered superfluous (as a footnote to the story suggests and two much later texts, "Undr" and "The Book of Sand," make clear) since a single book can hold all others. This is the idea behind "An Examination of the Work of Herbert Quain" of 1941, in which an imaginary writer invents an infinite series of novels based on the notion of geometrical progression. Once, after noting that we read now Dante in ways that he couldn't have imagined, far beyond the "four levels" of reading outlined in Dante's letter to Can Grande della Scala, Borges recalled an observation by the ninth century mystic Scotus Erigena. According to the author of *On the Divisions of Nature*, there are as many readings of a text as there are readers; this multiplicity of readings, Erigena compared to the hues on the tail of a peacock. In text after text, Borges explored and laid out the laws of this peacock range.

Such renewals and subversions did not make him popular with everyone. When his first stories appeared in France, Etiemble ironically remarked that Borges was "a man to be eliminated," since his work threatened the whole notion of authorship. Others, especially in Latin America, felt offended by his lack of documentary interest, his avoidance of literature as reportage. Beginning as early as 1926, Borges's critics accused him of many things: of not being Argentine ("being Argentine," Borges had quipped, "is an act of faith"); of suggesting, like Oscar Wilde, that art is useless; of not requiring literature to have a moralizing or pedagogic purpose; of being too fond of metaphysics and the fantastic; of preferring an interesting theory to the truth; of pursuing philosophical and religious ideas for their aesthetic value; of not being politically engaged (in spite of his strong stance against Peronism and Fascism) or of tolerating the wrong side (as when he shook hands with both Videla and Pinochet, acts for which he later apologized, and signed his name to a plea for the *desaparecidos*). He dismissed these criticisms as attacks on his opinions ("the least important aspect of a writer") and politics ("the most miserable of human activities"). He said that no one could ever accuse him of being in favour of Hitler or Perón.

He talks about Perón but tries not to mention his name. He tells me that he had heard that in Israel, when someone tries out a new pen instead of signing his name, he writes the name of the ancient enemy of the Hebrews, the Amalekites, and then crosses it out, thousands of years later. Borges says he will continue to cross out Perón's name whenever he can. According to Borges, after Perón came into power in 1946, anyone who wanted an official job was required to belong to the Peronist Party. Borges refused and was transferred from his position as assistant librarian in a small municipal branch to inspector of poultry at a local market. According to others, the transfer was less injurious but equally absurd: to the Municipal Apiary School. Whatever the case, Borges resigned. After his father's death, in 1938, Borges and his mother depended entirely on his librarian's salary and, after his resignation, he had to find another way of earning a living. In spite of his shyness, he started to give public lectures and developed a style and a lecturing voice that he still uses.

I watch him prepare for a talk he has to give at the Italian Institute of Culture. He has memorized the whole thing, line after line, paragraph after paragraph repeated until every hesitancy, every apparent search for the right word, every happy turn of phrase is soundly rooted in his mind. "I think of my public speeches as the shy man's revenge," he says, laughing.

In spite of his essential humanism, there were times when his prejudices made him surprisingly and horribly peurile. For instance, he voiced on occasion a senseless, commonplace racism that suddenly transformed the intelligent, keen reader into a momentary dolt who offered, as proof of a black man's inferiority, the lack of a culture of universal importance. In such cases, it was useless to argue with him or attempt to excuse him.

The same was true in the realm of literature, where it was easier to put his opinions down to questions of sympathy or
whim. One could construct a perfectly
acceptable history of literature consisting
only of the authors Borges rejected: Austen,
Goethe, Rabelais, Flaubert (except the first
chapter of *Bouvard et Pécuchet*), Calderón,
Stendhal, Zweig, Maupassant, Boccaccio,
Proust, Zola, Balzac, Galdós, Lovecraft,
Edith Wharton, Neruda, Alejo Carpen-
tier, Thomas Mann, García Márquez,
Amado, Tolstoi, Lope de Vega, Lorca,
Pirandello . . . He wasn't interested (after
the experiments of his youth) in novelty
for the sake of novelty. He said that the
writer should not have the impoliteness of
surprising the reader. He sought in literature conclusions that were both astonishing and obvious. Recalling that Ulysses,
tired of prodigies, wept for love at the sight
of his green Ithaca, he concluded: "Art

should be like that Ithaca—of green eternity, not of prodigies."

New Year's Eve 1967, in a sultry and noisy Buenos Aires, I find myself near Borges's apartment and decide to give him my best wishes. He is at home. He has drunk a glass of cider at the apartment of Bioy and Silvina, and now he sits at home, working. He pays no attention to the whistles and petards, "people celebrating dutifully as if once again the end of the world were near," because he is composing a poem. His friend Xul Solar told him, many years ago, that what you do on New Year's Eve reflects your activity for the months to come, and Borges has followed this admonition faithfully. Every New Year's Eve he superstitiously begins a text so that the following year may grant him further writing. "Will you jot down a few words for me?" he asks. Like so many of his texts, the words compose a list, since, he says, "making lists

is one of the oldest activities of the poet": "El
bastón, las monedas, el llavero . . ." I no longer
remember the other objects lovingly brought
to mind, leading up to the last sentence: "No
sabrán nunca que nos hemos ido."

The last time I read for him was in 1968; his
choice for the evening was Henry James's
story "The Jolly Corner." The last time I
saw him was years later, in Paris, in the base-
ment breakfast room of l'Hôtel in Paris,
in 1985. He talked despondently about
Argentina and said that though you called
a place your own and said you lived there,
you really mean a group of a few friends
whose company define that or any other
place as yours. He talked about the cities
he thought of as his—Geneva, Montevideo,
Nara, Austin, Buenos Aires—and wondered
(he wrote a poem about this) in which one
he would die. He discarded Nara, in Japan,

where he had "dreamed of the terrible image of Buddah, whom I had not seen but touched." "I don't want to die in a language I cannot understand," he said. He said he looked forward to the end. He said he couldn't understand Unamuno, who had written that he longed for immortality. "Someone who longs to be immortal must be crazy, eh?"

In the case of Borges, it was his work, his material, the stuff on which his universe was made that was immortal, and for that reason he himself did not feel the need to seek an everlasting existence. "The number of themes, of words, of texts, is limited. Therefore nothing is ever lost. If a book is lost, then someone will write it again, eventually. That should be enough immortality for anyone," he said to me once when he was talking about the destruction of the Library of Alexandria.

There are writers who attempt to put the world in a book. There are others, rarer, for whom the world *is* a book, a book that they attempt to read for themselves and for others. Borges was one of these writers. He believed, against all odds, that our moral duty was to be happy, and he believed that happiness could be found in books, even though he was unable to explain why this was so. "I don't know exactly why I believe that a book brings us the possibility of happiness," he said. "But I am truly grateful for that modest miracle." He trusted the written word, in all its fragility, and through his example, he granted us, his readers, access to that infinite library which others call the Universe. He died on 14 June 1986, in Geneva, the city in which he had discovered Heine and Virgil, Kipling and De Quincey, and where he first read Baudelaire whom he then loved (he learned *Les Fleurs du mal* by heart) and now abominated. The last book he asked to be read to him, by a German-speaking nurse at the hospital, was *Heinrich*

von Ofterdingen by Novalis, which he had
first read in his Geneva adolescence.

But these are not memories; they are memories of memories of memories, and the
events that sparked them have vanished
away, leaving only a few images, a few
words, and even those I can't be certain
were as I think I remember them. "I am
moved by small wisdoms that are lost at
every death," Borges wrote wisely in his
youth. The boy who climbed the stairs is
lost somewhere in the past, and so is the
wise old man who liked stories. He enjoyed
old metaphors—time as a river and life as
a voyage and a battle—and that battle and
that voyage are now over for him, and the
river has washed those evenings of everything except the literature which (he would
quote Verlaine) is what is left after that

which is essential, and always beyond the grasp of words, has had its say.

The reading comes to an end. Borges makes one last comment—on Kipling's youth, on Heine's simplicity, on the endless complexity of Góngora, so different from the artificial complexity of Gracián, on how there is no description of the pampa in Martín Fierro, on the music of Verlaine, on the goodnaturedness of Stevenson. He remarks that every writer leaves two works: the written work and the image of himself, and that both creations pursue one another till the end. "A writer can only hope to be satisfied with bringing at least one to a worthy conclusion, eh?" And then, with a smile: "But with how much conviction?" He stands up. He offers for the second time the anodyne hand. He walks me to the door. "Good night," he says. "Till tomorrow, eh?" without expecting an answer. Then the door closes slowly.

NOTES

de Nortumbria y de Mercia/ Antes de ser
Haslam o Borges." ("Al iniciar el estudio de
la gramática anglosajona" in *El Hacedor*)

29   "Con el tiempo, todo poema se convierte
en una elegía."

30   "Soy un lector hedónico: jamás consentí
que mi sentimiento del deber interviniera
en afición tan personal como la adquisición
de libros." ("Paul Groussac" in *Discusión*)

30   "pertenecientes al Emperador" (. . .) "que de
lejos parecen moscas" ("El idioma analítico
de John Wilkins" in *Otras Inquisiciones*)

34   "una larga metáfora del insomnio" (Fore-
word to *Artificios*, in *Ficciones*)

34   "Mi memoria, señor, es como vaciadero de
basuras." ("Funes el memorioso" in *Ficciones*)

38   "Once again you feel the bush and valley
still with the glimmer of the fog."

40   "[The swan] floats and floats on the quiet
lake/ That in dreams awaits those who are
sad/ Where a golden gondola lies waiting/
For the bride of Ludwig of Bavaria."

44   A literal translation: No one saw him dis-
embark in the unanimous night, no one
saw the canoe made of reeds sink into the

sacred mud, but a few days later no one ignored that the taciturn man came from the South and that his homeland was one of the infinite villages upstream, in the rough flank of the mountain, where the Zend tongue is not contaminated by Greek and where leprosy is infrequent." ("Las ruinas circulares" in *Ficciones*)

47 "To a Young Poet/It's useless for you to foster/ Any idea of advancement/ Because even if you write huge quantities/ Borges will have written it first." (Unpublished)

50 "Víctor Hugo, che, ese gallego insoportable; el lector se ha ido y él sigue hablando."

50 "Faltaron tantos, que si faltaba uno más ya no cabía."

56 "Bioy Casares había cenado conmigo esa noche y nos demoró una vasta polémica sobre la ejecución de una novela en primera persona, cuyo narrador omitiera o desfigurara los hechos e incurriera en diversas contradicciones, que permitieran a unos pocos lectores—a muy pocos lectores—la adivinación de una realidad atroz o banal." ("Tlön Uqbar, Orbis Tertius" in *Ficciones*)

69 "That dark light that falls from the stars." Le Cid, IV, 3

82 "The cane, the coins, the keyring [. . .] will never know that we have gone."

85 "Me comueven las menudas sabidurías/ que en todo fallecimiento se pierden." ("La noche que en el Sur lo velaron" in *Cuaderno San Martín*)

ALBERTO MANGUEL

Alberto Manguel was born in Buenos Aires in 1948, and is now a Canadian citizen. After spending his childhood in Israel, where his father was the Argentine ambassador, he attended school in Argentina. In 1968 he left for Europe and for the next few years, with the exception of one year back in Buenos Aires where he worked as a journalist for the newspaper *La Nación*, he lived in Spain, France, England and Italy earning an itinerant living as a reader for various publishing companies. In the mid-seventies he was offered (and accepted) a job as assistant editor at Les Editions du Pacifique, a publishing company in Tahiti. In 1982, after the publication of *The Dictionary of Imaginary Places* (written with Gianni Guadalupi), he moved to Canada.

He has edited a dozen anthologies of short stories on themes ranging from fantastic to erotic literature, and has written several books of fiction and non-fiction, among them *A History of Reading*, translated into over twenty-five languages; *Into the Looking-Glass Wood: Essays on Words and the World*; *Reading Pictures*; and the novel *News from A Foreign Country Came*. He contributes regularly to newspapers and magazines around the world.